THE
MILLENNIUM

COMMUNICATION

A Pictorial History of the
Past One Thousand Years

Sue Hamilton

AB&DO
Daughters

Visit us at
www.abdopub.com

Published by ABDO Publishing Company, 4940 Viking Drive, Edina, MN 55435.
Copyright ©2000 by Abdo Consulting Group, Inc. International copyrights reserved in all countries. No part of this book may be reproduced in any form without written permission from the publisher.

Printed in the United States.

Contributing Editors: Bob Italia, Tamara Britton, Kate Furlong
Art Direction: Pat Laurel, John Hamilton

Cover photos: AP/Wideworld Photos, Corbis
Interior photos: AP/Wideworld Photos, Corbis

Library of Congress Cataloging-in-Publication Data

Hamilton, Sue L., 1959-
    Communication/Sue Hamilton
        p. cm. -- (The millennium)
    Includes bibliographical references and index.
    Summary: A pictorial history of developments in communication over the last millennium.
    ISBN 1-57765-359-9
    1. Communication--History--Pictorial works--Juvenile literature. [1. Communication--History.] I. Title. II. Millennium (Minneapolis, Minn.)

P91.2 .H27 2000
302.2'09--dc21

99-054105

CONTENTS

Introduction 4

Before the Millennium 6

1000 to 1100 8

1100 to 1200 9

1200 to 1300 10

1300 to 1400 11

1400 to 1500 12

1500 to 1600 13

1600 to 1700 14

1700 to 1800 15

1800 to 1850 16

1850 to 1875 18

1875 to 1900 20

1900 to 1910 22

1910 to 1920 24

1920 to 1930 26

1930 to 1940 28

1940 to 1950 30

1950 to 1960 32

1960 to 1970 34

1970 to 1980 36

1980 to 1990 38

1990 to 2000 40

Communication Milestones 42

Glossary 44

Internet Sites 47

For Further Reading 47

Index 48

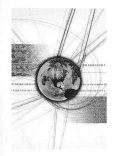

INTRODUCTION

The word *communication* comes from the Latin word *communicare*, which means *to share*. The sharing of ideas and information began with the earliest humans, who drew on cave walls and spoke the first words.

As the earliest civilizations developed, so too did the need for better ways to communicate. Writing gave humans a better way to store and transfer knowledge. Printing gave the masses access to the written word, and the global spread of information began.

Toward the end of the past millennium, electronics became the driving force of new communication devices. The Information Age had begun.

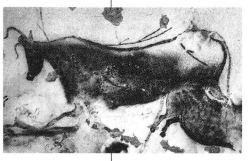

This image of a red cow (above), in France's Lascaux Grotto, was painted sometime between 15,000 and 13,000 B.C.

Language

Primitive forms of language became necessary when humans acted together to accomplish a task such as hunting or making pottery.

Many different languages were spoken and written at the end of the millennium. Some languages, such as English, use letters to represent sounds. The letters are combined to make words. Other languages, such as Chinese, use characters to represent each word in their vocabulary. One needs to know 2,000 to 3,000 Chinese characters in order to read a magazine article.

Writing

As people explored the world, they sought new ways to communicate over long distances. Ancient Egyptians created writing on clay tablets, and even developed clay "envelopes" for their messages. Messengers carried information cross country, and smoke and drums signaled information. Homing pigeons transported messages in early postal systems. Writing instruments and paper improved.

Sumerians marked pictographic symbols in soft pieces of clay with a pointed reed (left). The clay tablets were then baked to make them hard. The Sumerian writing system is known as cuneiform.

Technology

The printing press was the first great mass communication device of the millennium. It provided books, newspapers, and magazines to people throughout the world.

Late in the millennium, the advent of electronics would lead to the modern communication methods of satellite transmissions, personal computers, email, and Internet access.

Johannes Gutenberg's fifteenth century printing press revolutionized the printing process.

Newspapers have provided information since the 1600s.

Personal computers appeared in the 1970s.

Pagers and cellular telephones became a quick and easy way to communicate at the end of the millennium.

Access to the World Wide Web began in 1992.

Direct broadcast satellite (DBS) service began in 1994.

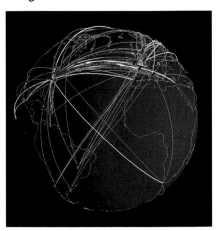

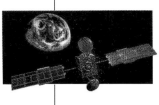

BEFORE THE MILLENNIUM

Ancient people used many different forms of communication to express themselves. As technology slowly improved, so did their ability to communicate. Communication methods evolved from cave paintings to complex written languages. The invention of paper improved written communication, and early postal systems allowed messages to be communicated over long distances.

Cave Paintings

Primitive paintings on cave walls (right) are the earliest documentation of human communication. These pictures convey the beliefs and rituals of prehistoric society.

Writing

Cuneiform was a way of writing used by the ancient peoples of the Middle East. Wedge-shaped strokes were inscribed on clay, stone, metal, wax, and other materials.

The earliest examples of cuneiform date from 3000 B.C. and were written by the Sumerians of southern Mesopotamia and Chaldea. Originally, each symbol stood for a word. For example, a starlike symbol represented the word *god*.

A cuneiform tablet from Sumer, around 2100 B.C.

The ancient Egyptians used a form of writing called hieroglyphics. The oldest hieroglyphics are from about 3000 B.C. Modern people did not understand these Egyptian writings until the discovery of the Rosetta Stone (below, right) in 1799. The stone contained three different writing systems. French linguist and historian Jean-François Champollion recognized one of the writing systems. Champollion deciphered the stone and discovered the key to translating ancient Egyptian writings.

Paper

Ancient people used many different surfaces to write on, including clay, tree bark, and stone blocks. In the third millennium B.C., Egyptians began writing on papyrus, a material made from the stalk of the papyrus plant. It was flexible, light, durable, and could be rolled into scrolls. Some of the oldest surviving Egyptian papyrus writings, known as the Book of the Dead, were written in the third millennium B.C.

The ancient Greeks are credited with the creation of parchment in the second century B.C. Parchment is made from animal skins that have been specially prepared for writing.

In A.D. 105, Ts'ai Lun, a court official to the Chinese emperor, developed the first modern paper. Ts'ai's paper was made from tree bark, hemp waste, old rags, and fish nets. Its writing surface was superior to silk, the main writing surface used in China at the time.

A papyrus scroll from Egypt, written around 1000 B.C.

The Old Testament Book of Esther from the Bible, written in Hebrew in the 8th Century A.D.

Postal System

Ancient empires used postal systems and messengers to deliver information over long distances. The oldest reference to a postal system is from Egypt in about 2000 B.C.

China's Chou Dynasty created the post and relay system around 1000 B.C. In this system, posts were set up at regular intervals. A messenger on horseback would carry the mail from his post to the next and pass the letters on to another rider, who would carry them to the next post.

By the sixth century B.C., Darius of Persia had established a complex postal system spanning a distance of 1,600 miles (2,574 km). The Romans also had a highly developed system for relaying messages called the *cursus publicus*. In the Americas, the Incan and Mayan Empires used foot messengers and relay stations.

The ancient Greeks used foot messengers (right). In 490 B.C., a Greek soldier ran from Marathon to Athens to bring news of the Athenian victory over the Persians.

1000 TO 1100

The Egyptians, Chinese, Greeks, and Romans had made remarkable advancements in communication. This progress continued with the development of accounting methods, as well as an important advancement in printing.

Record Keeping

The ancient Incas of Peru used a system of knotted and colored strings called *quipu* to keep track of population, food inventories, and production from their gold mines.

Each knot in a quipu (above) represented a numerical unit.

Writing

The Mayas of Mexico recorded their history and traditions in hieroglyphics. Some of the hieroglyphics were put into a book format called a codex. Codices were written on paper made from fig-tree bark and had covers made of jaguar skin.

Only four Mayan codices have survived. The oldest one, called the Dresden Codex (right), dates from between the eleventh and twelfth centuries A.D.

A modern reproduction of Pi Sheng's moveable type

Printing

In about 1041, Chinese alchemist Pi Sheng invented movable type made of clay and glue hardened by baking.

Each firebaked clay piece was an individual character that could be picked up and arranged in any order on an iron plate coated with wax. These were then covered in ink and could be used to make printed materials.

When finished, the plate could be heated and the type would come out.

1100 TO 1200

Advancements in printing continued with the introduction of the papermaking process from the East to the West. And in the East, a primitive postal system began.

Postal System
The twelfth-century Mongol ruler Genghis Khan created an early postal system using homing pigeons. The conqueror set up a pigeon relay system to communicate messages across his vast empire from China to Russia.

Paper
Although papermaking had gone on in China for many years, the art was introduced into Europe by the Moors of northern Africa, who had gained the secret from Chinese prisoners. The first paper created in Europe was made in Játiva, Spain, in 1151. The craft soon spread throughout Europe.

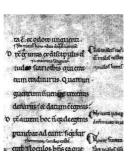

During the 1100s, vellum was also a commonly used writing surface. This is a vellum leaf from a twelfth century Latin manuscript found in Switzerland.

Signals
Smoke signals were still an important part of long-distance communication.

1200 TO 1300

With the written word becoming increasingly available, individuals began writing letters to each other. This new form of communication prompted the need for organized postal delivery and refinements in paper production.

Writing

Around A.D. 1200, monks in European monasteries began to communicate with others by sending letters. Monks were among the few people who could read and write at the time.

During the thirteenth century, the University of Paris (above) began its own messenger service.

Postal System

Beginning in about 1290, the Taxis family, originally from Milan, Italy, began a private postal service that grew to cover all of Europe. Their system of postal routes continued into the nineteenth century, and came to employ about 20,000 carriers. They are remembered as having the best private postal system in Europe.

When the Italian explorer Marco Polo visited China in the late thirteenth century, he found that Emperor Kublai Khan had developed an advanced postal system (right). According to Polo, it had 300,000 horses and posts every 25 to 30 miles (40 to 48 km) on the most traveled roads.

Paper

In the thirteenth century, Italian papermakers began adding watermarks to paper. Watermarks may show a company or paper name.

1300 TO 1400

Business people, students, families, and friends in the fourteenth century needed to devise methods to relay more information to more people. Around the same time period, a single document could be distributed for use by many different people.

Writing

By the beginning of the fourteenth century, universities had been established in Paris, Bologna, Padua, Ghent, Oxford, and Cambridge. These centers of learning created new demands for books, most of which were locked away in monasteries. So, two new kinds of occupations developed: stationers and book copiers.

Stationers provided paper and book copiers provided libraries of books that were available for students to copy. When students needed text for their classes, they would go to the stationers and copy them by hand. Or they could pay a book copier to copy the book for them.

A monk copies a page of a manuscript in a monastic scriptorium.

Libraries

In the fourteenth century, King Charles V of France (left) opened the *Bibliothèque du Roi* or Royal Library (right). This library became the *La Bibliothèque Nationale de France*, the national library of France.

11

1400 TO 1500

Great advancements in printing were made in the 1400s. Pi Sheng's moveable type was perfected, and color was added to printed pages. These developments, along with printing books in different languages, introduced the concept of the printed word as entertainment as well as communication.

Printing

In about 1455, Johannes Gutenberg (left) printed the Gutenberg Bible (right). It was the first book made from moveable metal type, oil-based ink, and a press similar to that used in wine making.

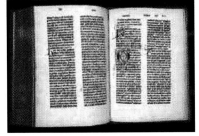

German businessman Johann Fust lent Gutenberg money to develop his printing process. When Gutenberg couldn't pay back the money, Fust sued him and received some of Gutenberg's printing equipment. The settlement included the type for the Bible and a new project Gutenberg had been working on called a Psalter.

Fust and his son-in-law Peter Schöffer used the materials they received from Gutenberg to publish the Psalter in 1457. The Psalter ran multiple color inks in the same press run. It is the first example of color printing.

The Psalter (above) had two-color initial letters.

In 1474, William Caxton translated a popular French romance into English. This book, *The Recuyell of the Historyes of Troye,* is the first book printed in English. Up to this point, most books were printed in Latin. With Caxton's success, books suddenly became printed in the language of the common people.

William Caxton demonstrates his printing press (left). A sample from Caxton's translation of The Recuyell of the Historyes of Troye *(right).*

1500 TO 1600

In the sixteenth century, long-distance communication by signal remained as it had for thousands of years. People were reading and writing more than ever before, and the process of printing books continued to evolve.

Signals

The British built a line of beacons that stretched from Portsmouth to London. In 1588, these signal houses warned Londoners of the approach of the Spanish Armada. This early-warning system allowed them enough time to gather forces and defeat the Spanish invaders.

This signal beacon on Frodsham Hill in Cheshire was erected to celebrate 400 years since the defeat of the Spanish Armada in 1588.

Printing

The operations of type design and manufacturing were slowly separated from the responsibilities of the printer. By the middle of the sixteenth century, a number of typefounders were in business for themselves.

A woodcut illustration shows a sixteenth century printing office. The compositor's case has only twenty-three characters since the j, u, and w were not in common use.

The typefounder in this illustration is at the far right.

1600 TO 1700

In the seventeenth century, people took advantage of new technology to improve long-distance communication. Postal delivery systems continued to evolve, and people developed tools to improve communication between themselves.

Newspapers

In 1605, Abraham Verhoeven of Antwerp published the *Nieuwe Tijdingen*. It was the first European newspaper.

Signals

In 1608, Dutchman Hans Lippershey created the first telescope. In 1609, Italian astronomer Galileo Galilei improved upon its design. The telescope was an important part of signaling systems. It helped people see signals from great distances, which sped up transmission time.

Postal System

In 1639, the first American postal service was established in the colony of Massachusetts.

Hearing Aids

The world's first hearing aid, called the ear trumpet, was invented in the second half of the seventeenth century. The ear trumpet was a cone-shaped device that magnified sound. To use the ear trumpet, the listener put the small end of the cone into his or her ear, and the speaker talked into the large end.

A man and girl use an ear trumpet to communicate with each other (left).

1700 TO 1800

Developments in printing continued with a new printing process and advancements in papermaking. The long-distance communication method of signaling was improved to relay specific written messages, and pioneers improved interpersonal communication between individuals with different abilities.

Postal System

Benjamin Franklin (above, right) became the first postmaster general, appointed by the Continental Congress in 1775. Although Americans had won their freedom from British rule, they maintained some of the British postal laws.

Sign Language

In the mid-eighteenth century, Abbé Charles-Michel de l'Epeé created the first single-hand manual alphabet. This system improved the education of deaf students, allowing them to communicate by using a standard language system.

Signals

French engineer Claude Chappe built a long-distance signaling system. It consisted of tall towers that had posts with movable arms on top. Each arm position stood for specific letters and words, and could be seen through a telescope from the next tower. Chappe's system was first used in 1794. It was replaced by the more efficient telegraph in about 1850.

Chappe's system (below) ran from Lille to Paris. The message could travel this 144-mile (232 km) distance in two minutes.

Printing

In 1798, Alois Senefelder of Germany developed a printing process known as lithography. This process is based on the fact that water and grease do not mix. By drawing on limestone with a grease crayon and applying ink, the ink stays on the crayon lines but washes away from the rest. Paper is then pressed onto the drawing and a lithograph (right) is produced.

Paper

In 1798, French inventor Nicholas-Louis Robert created the first machine for making a continuous roll of paper. The machine used a continuous flow of raw wood pulp moving along a wire mesh belt. The pulp was squeezed and heated between rollers to remove the water and dry the paper. It was then rolled up into a big reel.

A modern web press with a roll of paper

1800 TO 1850

The printing process continued to evolve with the further development of the printing press. Long-distance communication was improved with a new signaling device and a new electronic signal. Interpersonal communication was enhanced with a new method of communication for people who could not see. And a new machine made pictures.

Braille

In 1829, Louis Braille created a system of raised dots that represented letters, developing a way for blind people to read. This simple, yet remarkable system remained in use at the end of the millennium.

Printing

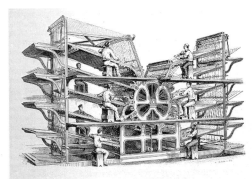

In 1814, the first workable cylinder press (left)—developed by Friedrich Koenig and Andreas Bauer—was put into service at the *Times* in London. A cylinder was rolled over stationary plates of inked type. The cylinder then made an impression on paper. This eliminated the need for making impressions directly from the type plates, which were heavy and difficult to maneuver. The cylinder press worked four times faster than previous presses.

In 1846, Richard M. Hoe created the rotary printing press (right). Type was locked in a large cylinder while paper sheets were fed to each of the small impression cylinders surrounding it, further increasing printing speed.

Photography

French inventor Joseph Nicéphore Niepce created a photograph of the courtyard of his house in 1826. It is the first surviving permanent photo known. Three years later, he formed a partnership with French painter Louis Jacques Mandé Daguerre (left).

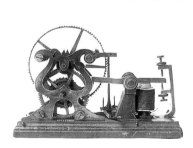

This daguerreotype of the U.S. Capitol building was taken in 1846 (left). Daguerreotypes were taken with cameras like the one below.

Niepce died in 1833, before the photographic process was perfected. In 1839, Daguerre (left) went on to develop a photograph made from a silver or silver-lined copper plate. His photographs, referred to as daguerreotypes, became the photographic standard for decades.

The Telegraph

British inventors Sir Charles Wheatstone and Sir William F. Cook and American inventor Samuel Morse (below, right) invented the telegraph (below) in 1837.

Morse also invented a telegraph communication system called Morse Code. It was made up of a series of long and short electrical impulses, referred to as dots and dashes. Each electrical impulse represents a letter or number. The pulses were sent between telegraphic machines.

Newspapers

In 1848, six New York newspapers formed the Associated Press (AP). AP cut down on the cost of gathering national news. It went on to become the largest news service in the world.

1850 TO 1875

Long-distance communication was expanded by an exciting, dangerous method of postal delivery that served the western United States. Electronic signaling was expanded to communicate farther than ever before. The printing press continued to improve, and a new machine allowed people to write quickly with the touch of a finger.

The Pony Express

From April 1860 until October 1861, the Pony Express was a mail delivery service that featured 80 riders, 500 thoroughbred horses, and nearly 190 relay stations.

Pony Express men rode about 100 miles (161 km) a day. It was tough work, and the riders faced everything from Indian attacks to severe weather.

The Pony Express could deliver mail from Missouri to California in only 10 days, faster than any other method. Famous men such as Wild Bill Hickok and Buffalo Bill Cody were Pony Express riders, and their stories became famous accounts of adventures in the West.

Pony Express service ended when the transcontinental telegraph system was completed in October 1861.

Printing

In 1865, William Bullock introduced the rotary web-fed letterpress machine. The press could feed paper on a continuous roll and print both sides of the paper at once. It was first used by the *Philadelphia Ledger*.

In 1871, R. Hoe & Co. introduced an improved version of the web press that corrected many of the flaws of Bullock's machine. Hoe's press was first used at the New York *Tribune* with great success. The web press soon became an industry standard.

A modern web press fed by rolls of paper

The Typewriter

Many attempts had been made to develop a typewriter before American inventor Christopher Sholes succeeded. With fellow mechanics Carlos Glidden and Samuel Soulé, Sholes patented the first functional typewriter in 1867.

In 1873, the Remington Arms Company signed a contract to manufacture Sholes's typewriters. For the next hundred years, nearly every office in America would have one or more of these revolutionary tools.

On early typewriters, the keyboard was laid out alphabetically. But, when a typist struck keys next to each other, the bars often jammed. To solve this, Sholes developed a new keyboard layout in 1873. It is known as "QWERTY" after the letters in the upper left-hand corner of the keyboard. The keys used most often in English were placed far apart from each other, eliminating jams.

At first, typewriters printed only capital letters. But in 1878, Sholes added a shift key and placed a capital and lower case letter on each typing bar.

The QWERTY keyboard layout and shift key design were still used at the end of the millennium.

The Telegraph

In 1858, the first transatlantic telegraph cable was laid between Valentia, Ireland, and Bull's Bay, Newfoundland.

After initial success, corrosion soon caused the cable to break, and the service failed. But another try was made in 1866, and it enjoyed long-term success.

In 1867, E. A. Calahan of the American Telegraph Company invented the first stock telegraph printing instrument (right). He had the idea that stock prices might be made available through some form of telegraphy. The distinct sound of this telegraph printing instrument eventually earned it the name of "stock ticker."

Sailors deploy the transatlantic telegraph cable from a group of ships in the mid-Atlantic Ocean.

1875 TO 1900

Amazing achievements were realized when people had the ability to speak directly with others who were in different locations. A device to record the spoken word and a new writing instrument also improved interpersonal communication. A new device helped people who could not hear, and pictures were made to move.

The Telephone

Alexander Graham Bell (left), a Boston speech teacher, is credited with the invention of the telephone.

On March 10, 1876, Bell's assistant, Thomas Watson, was standing next to the receiver and clearly heard the first telephone message: "Mr. Watson, come here. I want you."

Alexander Graham Bell's first telephone

The Phonograph

Thomas Alva Edison (below, right) spoke the world's first recorded words, the poem *Mary Had a Little Lamb*. An astounding inventor with more than 1,000 patents, Edison created the first phonograph (below, left) in 1877.

Edison's phonograph used small cylinders covered in a thin coat of wax, onto which a needle recorded sound as a groove in the cylinder. To play the recording, a needle picked up the sound and sent it through headphones and later through a trumpet-shaped horn.

Hearing Aid

In 1880, R.G. Rhodes improved on the ear trumpet with another primitive hearing aid called the audiophone (left). The device was a thin sheet of hard rubber or cardboard placed against the teeth, which conducted vibrations to the auditory nerve.

The Camera

George Eastman (right) brought photography to the masses with several inventions in the late nineteenth century.

In 1884, Eastman patented the first film in roll form. In 1888, he made a simple-to-use Kodak box camera. In 1889, he manufactured a flexible, transparent film. He formed the Eastman Kodak Company in 1892 to mass-produce photographic equipment.

Eastman's slogan for the box camera (left) was "You push the button—we do the rest."

Writing

L.E. Waterman, a New York insurance agent, wanted a pen that worked well. So, in 1884, he patented a fountain pen with its own ink reservoir. Waterman developed a mechanism that allowed the ink to flow evenly while writing. His fountain pen remained Westerners' main writing tool until the ball-point pen was developed 70 years later.

The Linotype machine (below)

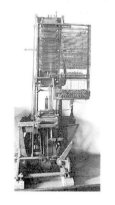

Printing

In 1884, Ottmar Mergenthaler patented the Linotype machine. It was a typesetting machine that cast a solid, one-piece line of type instead of individual characters. The machine dramatically decreased the amount of time needed to set type.

Motion Pictures

Thomas Alva Edison and his assistant William K.L. Dickson built a kinetoscope motion picture camera in 1891 (right). The kinetoscope showed an endless loop of film running past a magnifying screen. In April of 1894, the manufacturers of the kinetoscope, Raff & Gammon, opened the first kinetoscope parlor. The New York City parlor had 5 kinetoscopes and the admission was 25 cents.

1900 TO 1910

I n the first decade of the twentieth century, communication technology continued to improve. With the invention of the radio, human voices could carry messages across continents. Communication devices such as cameras, typewriters, and phonographs continued to improve in quality, making communication easier. Movie theaters opened in the U.S. and Europe, providing inexpensive news and entertainment.

Radio

In 1887, Heinrich Rudolf Hertz proved that electromagnetic waves travel at the speed of light. Hertz's discovery led to the creation of the modern radio.

Guglielmo Marconi (left), an Italian engineer, began experiments based on Hertz's discoveries. In 1894, Marconi invented wireless telegraphy, a form of telegraphy that is transmitted over radio waves and without connecting wires.

Marconi formed the Wireless Telegraph and Signal Company in 1897, improving his equipment. In 1901, he sent a transatlantic signal, the Morse Code signal for the letter *s*, from Cornwall, England, to Newfoundland, Canada.

From his experimental station at Brant Rock, Massachusetts, Reginald Fessenden broadcast the first radio program in 1906. He aired two songs, a poem, and a brief talk. Fessenden's broadcast was picked up by ships on the Atlantic hundreds of miles away.

Lee De Forest invented the Audion Vacuum Tube in 1906 (below, right). It provided the technology for live radio broadcasts. It was the type of vacuum tube used in all radio, radar, television, and computer systems until the transistor replaced it about 50 years later.

In August 1909, the *Arapahoe* became the first ship to use the radio distress call, S.O.S. Wireless operator T. D. Haubner radioed for help when his ship was in trouble off Cape Hatteras, North Carolina. Before this time, distress calls were "CQD." "CQ" stood for a general call and "D" for distress. S.O.S replaced CQD, simply because the three dots/three dashes/three dots signal was unmistakable.

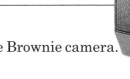

The Camera

In 1900, George Eastman introduced the Brownie camera. It sold for $1.

The Typewriter

Thomas Alva Edison patented the electric typewriter in 1872. In 1908, the Blickensderfer Typewriter Company built the first practical electric typewriter (left). Electric typewriters produced more uniform type than earlier typewriters had, and their light touch reduced operator fatigue.

Motion Pictures

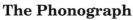

In the early twentieth century, Frenchman Charles Pathé (right) dominated motion picture production and distribution throughout the world. Pathé also introduced the world to newsreels. *Pathé Gazette* newsreels were first shown in Paris motion picture theaters in 1909.

In 1905, Americans Harry Davis and John P. Harris opened the first movie theater in Pittsburgh, Pennsylvania, and called it a nickelodeon. *Nickel* stood for the price of admission and *odeon* referred to the ancient Greek theaters.

The Phonograph

During the early 1900s, the Victor Talking Machine Company began using the phonograph advancements of Emile Berliner. Berliner had developed a stylus that moved horizontally rather than vertically and a new method for manufacturing flat phonographic discs. In Berliner's manufacturing process, discs were formed by pouring a mixture of shellac and plastic-like materials into a metal mold. Berliner's discs had more storage space and could be mass produced much easier than wax discs.

The Victor IV was manufactured by the Victor Talking Machine Co. from 1902 to 1920. It was originally priced from $50.00 to $57.50. This version came with a mahogany spear-tip horn, a double-spring motor, and an exhibition reproducer.

1910 TO 1920

Through the teens, the world became more connected as airmail and transcontinental telephone service made it faster and easier for people to communicate across long distances. The refinement of film created photographs of a higher quality. Radio quickly grew into an important form of communication as amateurs and professionals alike shared information over the airwaves.

Postal System

Airmail began officially in 1911 when French flier Henri Pequet transported mail in a biplane for 5 miles (8 km) from

Allahabad to Naini Junction in India. That same year, Gustave Hamel carried 25,000 letters and 90,000 postcards between Windsor and Hendon, England.

The United States Post Office opened its first regularly scheduled airmail service in 1918. Army pilots flew between Washington, D.C., and New York City. The first transcontinental route began in 1920 with service between New York City and San Francisco.

The Camera

Oskar Barnack (left) had the idea of reducing the format of negatives, and then enlarging the photographs after they had been exposed. As development manager at Leica in Germany, he put his theory into practice in 1914, creating the Ur-Leica (right). It was the world's first 35mm camera.

The first photos developed were of outstanding quality for the time. But World War I interrupted development, and Leica cameras did not go public for another decade.

Radio

Wireless radio had just become popular in the U.S. when the Radio Act of 1912 limited the frequency of private stations run by amateurs to 200 meters. The estimated number of amateur broadcasters declined. When the U.S. entered World War I in 1917, all amateurs were ordered to dismantle their transmitters and receivers. Radio use, other than by the military, was restricted.

In 1920, the shortwave radio was invented (left). These radio broadcasts are in the high-frequency range (3 - 30 MHz) and can travel around the world.

On the night of November 2, 1920, Frank Conrad and Donald Little broadcast returns of the Harding-Cox presidential election from a rooftop shack atop radio station KDKA in Pittsburgh, Pennsylvania (right). This, the first commercial radio broadcast, began a rush to set up stations across the country.

The Telephone

At 4:30 P.M. on January 25, 1915, Alexander Graham Bell and Thomas Watson conducted the first public transcontinental telephone conversation.

From New York, Bell spoke to Watson in San Francisco, repeating the first complete sentence he had transmitted by telephone almost 40 years before: "Mr. Watson, come here. I want you." By August, the first trials of transmitting speech across the Atlantic had begun.

1920 TO 1930

The Roaring '20s saw many changes in communication. Newspapers transmitted information over the recently developed teletype machines. Talkies ended the era of silent films. An increased number of automobiles led to the invention of traffic signals. News magazines and radio programs kept people informed.

Pagers

The Detroit Police Department used the first pager system in 1921.

The Telegraph

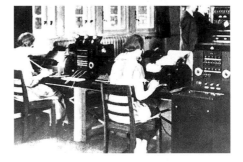

In the 1920s, the teletype machine became an important part of the telegraph system. The transmitter was a typewriter-like keyboard, where the message could be recorded. The receiver, a typewriter without a keyboard, printed the message on a tape or in paper form. News organizations around the world were the first to make use of this communication system.

In 1921, Western Union sent the first electronically-transmitted photograph.

Motion Pictures

In 1922, Robert J. Flaherty created the first movie documentary with *Nanook of the North* (left). Wanting to present true Eskimo life, Flaherty spent months shooting film in the Arctic.

In 1927, the *Jazz Singer* became the first movie to use a synchronized voice track. Music and words were recorded on large disks, then played to match the action on the screen.

The *Jazz Singer*'s star, Al Jolson, introduced audiences to talkies with the words, "You ain't heard nothing yet." These movies were an immediate hit, and within two years every studio had converted to talkies.

Signals

In the early twentieth century, bicycles, animal-powered wagons, and motor vehicles shared the roadways. Accidents were numerous. Inventor Garrett Augustus Morgan decided to help improve traffic safety.

In 1923, Morgan acquired a U.S. patent for the traffic signal (right). Morgan later had the technology patented in Great Britain and Canada.

The Morgan traffic signal was a T-shaped pole unit that featured three positions: stop, go, and an all-directional stop position that allowed pedestrians to cross streets safely.

Morgan's traffic management device was used throughout North America until it was replaced by the red, yellow, and green-light traffic signals currently used around the world.

Magazines

On March 3, 1923, Henry Luce and Briton Hadden introduced the first American news magazine, *Time*. The week's world events were summed up in 28 pages. The magazine continued to publish weekly editions into the new millennium.

Radio

By the mid-1920s, radio stations were broadcasting across the country. In 1924, the Eveready Hour became the first sponsored radio program. In 1929, engineer Paul Galvin invented the car radio (right).

Television

In 1927, Philo Farnsworth demonstrated the first television for potential investors by broadcasting the image of a dollar sign. Farnsworth received financial backing and applied for a patent. But ongoing patent battles with RCA prevented Farnsworth from earning his share of the million-dollar industry his invention created.

1930 TO 1940

During the 1930s, audiences could view movies in color. Ball-point pens and photocopiers made written communication easier to duplicate and more legible. Tape recorders allowed people to record sounds, and television made its first successful broadcast. Scientists began to work on the first computers.

Motion Pictures

In 1932, Walt Disney adopted the Technicolor process for the cartoon *Flowers and Trees*. Disney also used this colorization process on his first full-length feature cartoon, *Snow White*, in 1937. Technicolor was first used in John Whitney's 1934 Pioneer Picture, *Becky Sharp* (right).

Photography

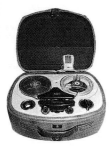

In 1931, Harold Edgerton invented the electronic flash. He used his knowledge and equipment to produce high-speed photography, like this photo of a hammer hitting a light bulb (left).

The Tape Recorder

In 1900, Valdimar Poulsen patented a method of reproducing sounds on magnetic wire. The first widespread use of magnetic recording occurred in 1934, when the German company Allgemeine Elektricitaets Gesellschaft (AEG) developed and manufactured the magnetophone (left). The Ampex corporation developed a machine patterned after the German one in 1948.

Photocopying

Working in a patent office in the 1930s, Chester Carlson found that he never had enough copies of patents around. With the help of German physicist Otto Kornei, Carlson worked on the problem of how to make copies easily.

One day in 1938, Carlson wrote the words "10-22-38 Astoria" on a microscope slide in India ink. Using a zinc plate covered in sulfur, he created "electrophotography," or the first photocopy.

Writing

Brothers Georg and Ladislao Biro invented a pen with a rolling ball tip in 1938. Their ball-point pen used waterproof ink, was almost unerasable, and could write on many different surfaces and in many different positions. Soon the ball-point pen became the universal writing tool.

Television

General Electric, Westinghouse, and RCA combined the efforts of inventors Philo Farnsworth, Allen B. Du Mont, and Vladimir Zworykin to produce the television. The first regular TV broadcasts began in 1939 with the broadcast of the opening ceremonies of the New York World's Fair.

To prove that no trickery was involved in creating the television broadcast images, RCA built a transparent television (right) so that World's Fair visitors could see the TV's inner workings. It was first displayed in the lobby of the RCA Pavilion and became the set most often associated with the beginning of the North American television age.

The Computer

In 1939, John Atanasoff and Clifford Berry of Iowa State College completed the prototype of the first digital computer (right), the Atanasoff-Berry Computer (ABC).

The full-scale version was the size of a desk, weighed 700 pounds (318 kg), used 300 vacuum tubes, and contained a mile (1.6 km) of wire. It could do about one operation every 15 seconds. But development of the ABC was soon stopped due to the onset of World War II.

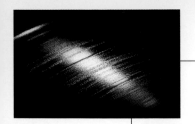

1940 TO 1950

The 1940s saw widespread growth of the television industry. Scientists programmed the first computer to do relatively quick and accurate mathematical calculations. The invention of Polaroid cameras allowed people to watch their pictures develop in a matter of seconds.

Television

The FCC authorized commercial television stations in 1941. New York's WNBT signed on the air on July 1 at 1:29 P.M. This historic event was the beginning of commercial television in the United States.

At 2:30 P.M. on the same day, WNBT again made history when 4,000 television sets were tuned to the station's first telecast, a game at Ebbets Field between Brooklyn and Philadelphia, followed by the Proctor & Gamble sponsored "Truth or Consequences."

The telecast also brought the first sponsor to the air, the Bulova clock company. Bulova paid $4 for the first commercial and $5 for the use of WNBT's facilities.

In April of 1942, the Defense Communications Board halted construction of new radio and television stations due to World War II. After the war, NBC began network television, linking together stations in Pennsylvania and New York. Television was expanding so rapidly that in 1948, the FCC declared a freeze on new stations to study frequency allocations. The freeze was not lifted until April of 1952.

In 1948, at the Bell Telephone Laboratories, physicists Walter Houser Brattain, John Bardeen, and William Bradford Shockley developed the transistor, a tiny device that could act as a switch or amplifier in an electric circuit (left). This tiny part replaced the costly, energy-inefficient, and unreliable vacuum tubes in hundreds of electronic machines, including newly developed computers. For their accomplishment, Brattain, Bardeen, and Shockley shared the 1956 Nobel prize for physics.

The Computer

Harvard University and IBM produced the Mark I (below) in 1944. It was over 50 feet long (15 m), 8 feet high (2 m), and weighed almost 5 tons (5.08 t), but it could solve an addition problem in less than a second, a multiplication problem in 6 seconds, and a division problem in 12 seconds.

Two years later, at the University of Pennsylvania, John Mauchly developed the ENIAC (right), which stood for "Electronic Numerical Integrator And Computer." It became the forerunner of the modern electronic computer.

The ENIAC weighed more than 60,000 pounds (27,216 kg) and used more than 18,000 vacuum tubes. Since it did not store programs, it had to be reprogrammed each time it was used.

The Camera

Edwin Herbert Land became interested in polarized light in his college years, eventually developing a new kind of polarizer he called Polaroid. He established his own corporation, Polaroid, in 1937. As with many others, his company turned from regular research in the 1940s to military efforts.

In 1947, he introduced the Polaroid Land camera, the first self-developing camera. Black and white pictures could be developed in a minute. It proved to be a very successful product.

1950 TO 1960

The speakerphone appeared in 1956. It allowed conference calls between groups at different locations.

Throughout the 1950s, communication technology continued to improve. Business began to use the first commercially-sold computers, and integrated microchips were invented. Satellites, the earliest form of space travel, provided the basis for future space communication systems. Video recorders were invented, and motion pictures demonstrated new special effects. Advancements in photocopiers made them practical in offices.

The Computer

Computer technology took giant steps forward in the early 1950s. The EDVAC (Electronic Discrete Variable Automatic Computer, left) finally stored the computer programs inside the computer.

Meanwhile, Remington Rand launched UNIVAC (Universal Automatic Computer), the first commercially available computer. Designed by Drs. Eckert and Mauchly, the team who invented the ENIAC computer, the U.S. Census Bureau received the first UNIVAC on March 31, 1951.

Transistors had to be soldered together, and the more complicated the connections, such as in a computer, the greater the chance of faulty wiring. In 1958, Jack St. Clair Kilby solved this problem by manufacturing the first integrated microchip (right). The chip consists of a collection of tiny transistors connected together when the microchip is manufactured.

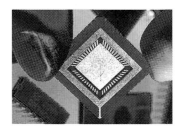

Pager

The term pager was used for the first time in 1959. It referred to a device developed by Motorola that could deliver a radio message directly to the person carrying the device.

Radio

The American company I.D.E.A. introduced the first transistorized radio, the Regency TR-1, on October 18, 1954. Transistors made radios small and portable.

Satellites

The world entered the space age when the U.S.S.R. launched its artificial satellites, beginning in 1957. The satellites were called Iskustvennyi Sputnik Zemli or "Sputnik" for short.

On October 4, 1957, *Sputnik 1* became the first man-made object to orbit the Earth. On November 3, 1957, *Sputnik 2* carried the dog Laika into orbit for seven days.

The U.S. launched its first satellite, *Explorer 1*, on January 31, 1958. This began the space race between the United States and the U.S.S.R.

The Video Recorder

On April 14, 1956, the National Association of Broadcasters was introduced to the first commercial videotape recorder by Ampex (right). It could record only in black and white. In 1959, Ampex, together with RCA, added color to video recording.

Motion Pictures

Motion pictures offered special entertainment to theater-goers of the early 1950s. Cinerama was released on September 30, 1952. Three projectors were used to fill the giant, curved screen, while full range stereophonic sound filled the theater.

Less than a year later, on April 9, 1953, Vincent

Price appeared in the first 3-D feature film by a major studio, Warner Brothers' *House of Wax* (left). Moviegoers wore special red and blue glasses to experience the three-dimensional effects of the film.

A Cinerama frame (above) is shown compared to the size of a normal frame of film.

The Photocopier

The Haloid company bought the electrophotography process in the 1950s. They developed a better-sounding name, xerography. The name came from the Greek word *xeros,* which means *dry,* and *graphos,* which means *writing.*

Their first photocopier was the Haloid Xerox Model A, introduced in 1949. But it was the Model 914 (right), introduced in 1957, that made Haloid Xerox a success. In 1961, the company changed its name to Xerox, and posted sales of nearly $60 million.

In 1963, Polaroid produced on-the-spot color photography with its first instant color film, Type 48.

1960 TO 1970

During the 1960s, communication systems grew even more far-reaching as satellites were proven to work as communication devices. The FCC introduced FM radio stations. Typewriters and telephones evolved into advanced forms. The U.S. Post Office introduced ZIP codes. Computers became smaller and easier to operate, while the U.S. government began to develop the Internet.

Satellites

In 1960, the United States sent a 100-foot (30-m) aluminized plastic balloon into orbit. *Echo I* (right) proved that satellites could be used as communications relays by reflecting, or echoing, radar and radio signals from transmitting stations down on Earth. The signals were then picked up by radio stations around the world.

Bell Labs, with AT&T, spent two years building the Telstar system (left), working in cooperation with NASA (National Aeronautics and Space Administration).

On July 10, 1962, NASA launched Telstar as the first orbiting international communications satellite system. Only two years later, Intelsat (International Telecommunications Satellite Organization) was formed.

Radio

In 1961, the FCC approved FM (Frequency Modulation) broadcasting. WEFM Chicago and WGFM Schenectady both started FM broadcasting on June 1.

The FM band in the United States runs from 88 MHz to 108 MHz. An FM radio signal is less sensitive to interference and static. Electrical disturbances, such as those created by thunderstorms, are picked up by AM (Amplitude Modulation) broadcast signals as static. With much less signal-to-noise, new FM stations grew rapidly.

The Typewriter

IBM introduced the Selectric typewriter in 1961. The Selectric had a replaceable typing ball that contained all the type characters.

Postal System

The Zoning Improvement Program (ZIP code) was put into place by the U.S. Post Office in 1963. Each of the ZIP code's five digits provide geographic information, improving postal delivery time and accuracy. The first three digits represent the area of the country and the last two digits represent the post office of the addressee.

The Telephone

Bell Labs continued its development of the telephone in the 1960s. Faster than the old rotary dials, touch-tone telephones were introduced in 1964 and grew to be the industry standard.

The Computer

In 1964, IBM rolled out the OS/360 (top, right), the first mass-produced computer operating system. Using the OS/360, all of the computers in the IBM 360 family could run any software program.

The following year, Digital Equipment introduced the minicomputer, the PDP-8. It was the world's first computer to use integrated circuit technology.

In 1968, Douglas Engelbart unveiled his newest creation: the "mouse" (bottom, right).

The Fax Machine

Though fax machines had been evolving since the late nineteenth century, they weren't widely used until the late 1960s. One of the first practical fax machines was the 1966 Xerox Telecopier 1.

The Internet

The United States military developed the Internet in the 1960s. By 1969, a network of university computers was created called ARPANET (Advanced Research Projects Agency Network).

Military researchers used electronic mail, or email, to send notes on projects, but soon discovered the system had a much greater communication potential.

1970 TO 1980

The innovations of the 1970s spread across many communication systems. Pagers allowed people to be reached at a moment's notice, and telephone lines used newly developed fiber-optic technology. Word processors made typing easier. VCRs became available on a wide scale. Computer technology expanded rapidly, making computers an increasingly important part of the business world.

Pager
The first modern pager, the Motorola Pageboy I, was introduced in 1974. It had no display and could not store messages.

The Telephone
In 1970, Corning Glass created a glass fiber so clear that it could communicate pulses of light. GTE and AT&T soon began experiments to transmit sound and image data using fiber optics, which transformed the communications industry.

The transaction telephone (above), introduced in 1976, could read the magnetic strip on credit cards.

The Typewriter
In 1971, Wang Laboratories brought the typewriter to a new level with the Wang 1200, the first word processor.

The VCR
Video cassette recorders (VCRs) entered homes in the 1970s. Consumers could watch one TV channel while videotaping another.

Two formats emerged: Sony Corporation's Betamax (left) and Matsushita's Video Home System (VHS). The two systems existed side-by-side. Eventually, VHS became the consumer standard, although Sony's Betamax format continued to be used by professionals.

The Computer

In the 1970s, a computer revolution began. Leading the way was the microprocessor, the supercomputer, and some young entrepreneurs who seized control of the personal computer market.

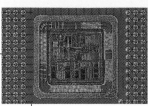

Billed as "a computer on a chip," Intel Corporation announced the first microprocessor (above), the Intel 4004, in 1971.

In 1971, Alan Shugart introduced the "memory disk," or "floppy disk" (left), an 8-inch (20 cm) plastic disk coated with magnetic iron oxide. The nickname "floppy" came from the disk's flexibility. The disks could hold computer programs and data.

In 1975, Bill Gates (right) and Paul Allen formed a partnership, known as Microsoft, to write computer software. They sold their first software to MIT, which had produced the Altair 8800, the first microprocessor-based computer.

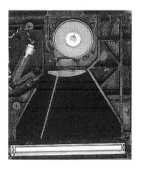

In 1976, IBM launched an electrophotographic computer printer called the laser printer. A focused laser beam (left) and a rotating mirror draw images on a photosensitive drum. The image is converted into an electrostatic charge, which attracts and holds the toner.

In 1976, Cray Research, Inc., introduced its first supercomputer, the Cray-1 (right). It could perform operations at a rate of 240,000,000 calculations per second.

In 1976, Steve Jobs (left), Stephen Wozniak, and Ron Wayne introduced the Apple I, the first low-cost microcomputer system. It included a built-in video terminal, and 4K bytes of RAM (expandable to 8K) on a single PC card. With an additional keyboard and monitor, people could develop their own programs, play games, or run BASIC.

1980 TO 1990

The 1980s saw an increased use of computer technology. The U.S. Post Office refined the ZIP code system, increasing the speed and accuracy of mail delivery. Cellular phone systems were established in the U.S., and the first CDs were sold. Camcorders allowed people to easily preserve events on video. Satellite communication systems grew in sophistication. Internet development continued to expand with the creation of Internet software.

The Computer

The computer industry presented the world with many great inventions in the 1980s. In 1981 came the IBM PC, the laptop computer, and the mouse. Apple computer introduced Engelbart's pointing device as a computer accessory in 1983. In 1984, the Apple Macintosh was introduced. That same year, a new computer operating system was introduced: Microsoft Windows.

The Postal System

In 1983, the U.S. Post Office introduced "ZIP + 4." This system added four digits to the five-digit ZIP code. The four new digits represented the block, apartment building, or office of the addressee.

The Telephone

AT&T introduced cellular communication in 1946. Japan established a cellular phone system in 1979. The United States established a system in 1983.

Wireless communication is called cellular because the system uses many base stations to divide large regions into smaller areas called cells. Cellular calls are transferred from base station to base station as a user travels from cell to cell. By 1985, cellular telephones were installed in cars.

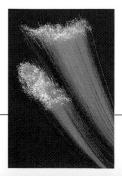

Fiber optic cables, made of glass or plastic, became widely used in the early 1980s. Voices, images, or data could be transmitted at nearly the speed of light.

The Compact Disc

Audio, video, and computer compact discs (CDs) were marketed to consumers in the 1980s.

James T. Russell had invented CDs in 1965. He was tired of his vinyl phonograph records wearing out. He developed a new process for recording, storing, and replaying information by laser.

A photosensitive platter records binary bits of information, while a laser reads the patterns. A computer converts the patterns into an electronic signal, which is then made audible or visible. Russell's CDs presented near-perfect playback that never wore out.

In 1983, companies like Phillips and Sony started a new industry standard by marketing music recorded on CDs. By the end of the decade, vinyl records were a thing of the past.

The Camcorder

The camcorder, a video camera and videocassette recorder, was introduced in 1984. This allowed for convenience and lighter-weight portability.

Satellites

Formed on the basis of an international treaty signed by President Kennedy, Intelsat brought many firsts to the world, including the 1969 transmission of Neil Armstrong's first walk on the moon.

In the 1980s, the Intelsat VI commercial satellite system first allowed broadcasters to transmit news feeds via the Intelsat system using small, easily transportable earth stations.

The Intelsat VI satellite system blasts off into space.

The Internet

The Internet continued to grow through the 1980s, becoming a worldwide collection of computers. In 1989, a group of physics researchers wanted to share their research with other researchers. So, they began devising new Internet software.

1990 TO 2000

By the 1990s, computers had become an important part of daily life. The Internet grew to become a major source of information for people in the Western world. Digital cameras took photography to new levels. Advanced television technology created a better picture, and movies could be played from discs rather than tapes.

The Internet

By 1990, Scientists could view, edit, and send documents to other scientists through special software on the World Wide Web. In 1991, the National Research and Education Network (NREN) was founded to create a way for any person or company to access the Internet.

The development of easy-to-use Web browsers, such as Mosaic in 1993 and Netscape Navigator in 1994, made the Internet accessible to the general public.

Throughout the 1990s, Web sites, Internet access, and email became an important part of communication.

The Computer

Apple Computer, Inc., introduced the Newton (left) in 1993. This hand-held computer allowed people to write notes with a stylus-type pen on a screen.

Though the Newton was not a success, a new generation of hand-held computers became popular by the end of the millennium. They helped people store notes, addresses, telephone numbers, important dates, and other information in an electronic device that could fit in a shirt pocket.

The Camera

In 1991, Kodak introduced the first digital camera system. It enabled photo journalists to take electronic pictures with a Nikon F-3 camera equipped by Kodak with a 1.3 megapixel sensor (left). It stored images on an optical disk instead of film.

Television

High Definition Television (HDTV) began development in the 1960s at Nippon Hoso and Kyokai, the Japanese Broadcasting Company. By the late 1990s, it was ready for introduction into the marketplace.

The main differences between the current analog TV and HDTV are picture quality and size. HDTV presents television programming in a wider format similar to that seen in a motion picture theater. HDTV also offers sharper, clearer, and better-sounding television.

Television stations must send out signals in both the current format and in digital form for some time to come. If the transition goes as planned, current analog televisions will no longer have any signals to receive in 15 years. Every broadcaster will have switched to HDTV.

DVD

In the late 1990s, Digital Video Disc (DVD) was introduced. The DVD format can store movies, computer programs, music, video games, and photos.

Because DVD is digital, it delivers superior picture clarity and color sharpness. With its multiple applications and huge storage capacity, the state-of-the-art DVD player is beginning to replace CDs, Compact Disc Read-Only Memory (CD-ROM), and VHS video machines.

COMMUNICATION

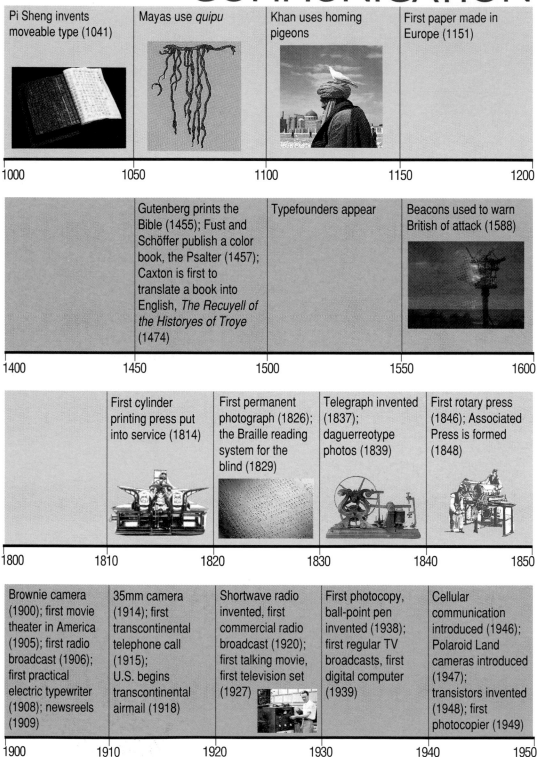

Pi Sheng invents moveable type (1041)

Mayas use *quipu*

Khan uses homing pigeons

First paper made in Europe (1151)

| 1000 | 1050 | 1100 | 1150 | 1200 |

Gutenberg prints the Bible (1455); Fust and Schöffer publish a color book, the Psalter (1457); Caxton is first to translate a book into English, *The Recuyell of the Historyes of Troye* (1474)

Typefounders appear

Beacons used to warn British of attack (1588)

| 1400 | 1450 | 1500 | 1550 | 1600 |

First cylinder printing press put into service (1814)

First permanent photograph (1826); the Braille reading system for the blind (1829)

Telegraph invented (1837); daguerreotype photos (1839)

First rotary press (1846); Associated Press is formed (1848)

| 1800 | 1810 | 1820 | 1830 | 1840 | 1850 |

Brownie camera (1900); first movie theater in America (1905); first radio broadcast (1906); first practical electric typewriter (1908); newsreels (1909)

35mm camera (1914); first transcontinental telephone call (1915); U.S. begins transcontinental airmail (1918)

Shortwave radio invented, first commercial radio broadcast (1920); first talking movie, first television set (1927)

First photocopy, ball-point pen invented (1938); first regular TV broadcasts, first digital computer (1939)

Cellular communication introduced (1946); Polaroid Land cameras introduced (1947); transistors invented (1948); first photocopier (1949)

| 1900 | 1910 | 1920 | 1930 | 1940 | 1950 |

MILESTONES

Italian papermakers add watermarks to paper; messengers at University of Paris; monks send letters	Postal system developed in China; Taxis family begins its postal service	King Charles V opens *Bibliothéque du Roi;* universities established in Europe	

1200	1250	1300	1350	1400

Verhoeven publishes first European newspaper, the *Nieuwe Tijdingen* (1605); Lippershey builds first telescope (1608); American postal system established (1639)	Ear trumpet invented		l'Epeé creates manual alphabet; Franklin appointed first American postmaster general (1775); Chappe builds telegraph towers (1794); Senefelder invents lithography (1798)

1600	1650	1700	1750	1800

First transatlantic telegraph cable laid (1858)	Pony Express (1860); U.S. transcontinental telegraph system (1861); web offset printing press (1865); typewriter, stock ticker (1867)	QWERTY layout for typewriter (1873); telephone (1876); phonograph (1877)	Audiophone (1880); fountain pen with reservoir, roll film, Linotype machine (1884); box camera (1888); flexible, transparent film (1889)	The kinetoscope (1891); Eastman Kodak Company (1892); wireless telegraphy (1894)

1850	1860	1870	1880	1890	1900

UNIVAC introduced (1951); transistor radio invented (1954); first satellite launched (1957); microchip invented (1958)	Computer "mouse" (1968); Telstar (1962); ZIP codes (1963); touch-tone telephones (1964); CDs (1965); desktop fax machine (1966); ARPANET (1969)	Fiber optics (1970); word processor, microprocessor, and floppy disk (1971); pagers (1974); supercomputers, laser printer, the Apple I (1976)	IBM PC, laptops (1981); U.S. "ZIP + 4" system (1983); Windows operating system, camcorders, the Macintosh (1984); first Internet software (1989)	The digital camera (1991); HDTV, DVD, and the World Wide Web

1950	1960	1970	1980	1990	2000

GLOSSARY

addressee - one to whom something is addressed.

alchemist - a scientist from the Middle Ages who attempted to turn common metals into gold, create a substance that would prolong life, and find a universal cure for disease.

amateur - a person who does something for fun rather than as a paid professional.

analog - a mechanism in which data are expressed in continuously variable physical quantities.

artificial satellite - a human-made object that orbits around Earth, the moon, or other heavenly bodies.

audible - a sound that is loud enough to be heard.

auditory nerve - the nerve that connects the inner ear with the brain.

BASIC (Beginner's All-purpose Symbolic Instruction Code) - a simplified language used for programming a computer.

beacon - a fire used for signaling that is usually on a hill, tower, or pole.

binary - made of two parts.

biplane - an airplane with two sets of wings that are usually placed one above the other.

byte - a unit of computer memory that is enough to represent one letter, number, or symbol.

commercial television - television that is supported by advertisers.

compositor - a person who sets type for printing.

computer program - a series of commands written in a programming language and coded into a computer that allow it to perform various functions.

corrosion - the process of wearing away slowly. It is usually caused by chemical action.

cuneiform - ancient, wedge-shaped writing.

decipher - to make out the meaning of something.

deploy - to spread out or arrange according to plan.

develop - to treat exposed photographic film or paper with chemicals in order to produce a visible image.

digital - a mechanism in which data are in quantities expressed as digits.

digits - the numbers from one to nine and the symbol 0.

disc - a storage medium that is read-only. Information can't be added or subtracted from a disc.

disk - a storage medium that can be rewritten. Information can be added or subtracted from a disk.

dismantle - to pull down or take apart.

documentary - a film that records information about something to preserve it for the future.

duplicate - to copy something.

electromagnetic waves - waves that are produced by variations in the intensity of electric and magnetic fields. Radio waves, visible light, and X rays are examples of electromagnetic waves.

electronics - devices that operate using electricity. Also, the study of physics that includes emission, behavior, and effects of electrons.

electrophotographic - a form of photography in which the images are produced by electricity and heat, instead of light and chemicals.

expose - to submit light-sensitive materials, such as photographic film, to light.

fax (facsimile) - a system of transmitting and reproducing images by means of signals sent over telephone lines.

fiber optics - thin, transparent fibers made of glass or plastic that transmit light down their entire length by internal reflection.

forerunner - something that precedes and indicates the approach of others like it.

geographic - belonging to a specific region.

hieroglyph - a character used in a language made of picture symbols.

high speed - photography that shoots frames at high speed to record movements that happen too fast to be seen under normal conditions.

homing pigeon - a racing pigeon that is trained to always return to its home.

India ink - a solid black pigment that, when suspended in water, makes an ink for writing and drawing.

innovation - a new idea, method, or device. Also, the introduction of something new.

integrated microchip - a group of electric components and their connections on a small piece of material such as silicon.

interference - the confusion of radio waves due to noise or another transmitter operating on the same frequency.

international - relating to or effecting two or more nations.

interpersonal - relations between people.

investor - a person who commits money to support a project in hopes of making more money.

laser - a powerful beam of light produced by using vibrating atoms or molecules between energy levels.

legible - clear and capable of being read.

linguist - a person who studies language.

mass production - to produce something in large quantities.

megapixel - a pixel is a small element that makes up an image like that on a TV screen. A megapixel is a pixel that is larger than normal.

microprocessor - a computer processor contained on an integrated microchip.

minicomputer - a small computer.

monastery - a place where people who have taken religious vows, usually monks, go to live.

mouse - a device that controls the movement of a computer's cursor and also selects functions.

negative - the images on film who pictures are printed from.

network television - a system of television stations owned by one company. Programs are broadcast on stations throughout the whole network.

newsreel - a short movie about current events.

optical disk - a disk with a plastic coating on which information is recorded digitally.

orbit - a circular path, or a path that makes one complete revolution around something.

patent - a written document that secures for an inventor exclusive rights to make, use, or sell his or her invention.

PC card - a card on which computer information is stored. Also, a card that has electronic circuit components for insertion into another device.

physicist - a person who studies the science of matter and energy and their interactions.

pictograph - an ancient drawing on a rock wall. Also, a symbol in a pictorial graphic language.

polarized light - a form of light in which the vibration of the waves is confined to a single plane or direction.

postmaster general - the person who is in charge of a post office.

potential - a possibility that could become a reality.

prototype - a model on which something is patterned, or the first full-scale, functional form of an object.

psalter - a collection of psalms for devotional or teaching purposes.

RAM (random-access memory) - the short-term memory on a computer's hard drive.

receiver - a device that converts electric impulses into sound.

refine - to improve or make perfect.

reservoir - a place in something where liquid is stored.

rotary dial telephone - a telephone that uses rotary pulses instead of touch-tone sound pulses.

scroll - a written document that is rolled up.

shellac - a partially solid substance that can be easily molded. Shellac is secreted by scale insects.

sophisticated - highly developed or complicated.

sponsor - one who pays for radio or television programming, usually in return for advertising time.

static - noise produced in a radio or television receiver by electrical disturbances. Also, the disturbances themselves.

stationary - fixed in station, course, or mode.

stylus - an instrument for writing, marking, or incising. Also, a slender rod with a rounded tip used to transmit vibrations from a record on a phonograph.

sulfur - a nonmetallic element.

supercomputer - a large mainframe computer used especially for scientific calculations.

synchronize - to make multiple things happen at the same rate in time.

tablet - a flat slab suited for or having an inscription.

talkie - a movie with a synchronized soundtrack.

Technicolor - a process that uses three different colors of film (red, blue, and yellow) to film a movie. The films are later combined into a single film that has the colors of the original movie scenes.

technology - the practical application of knowledge in a particular area.

telegraph - an apparatus for communicating long distances using electric transmission of coded signals over wires.

telegraphy - the use or operation of telegraph equipment.

thoroughbred - thoroughly trained or skilled. Also, something made from the best components.

transaction telephone - a telephone that sends information over wires.

transatlantic - crossing over or extending across the Atlantic Ocean.

transcontinental - crossing over or extending across a continent.

transistor - a solid-state electronic device used to control the flow of electricity in electronic equipment.

transmission - the passage of radio waves between the transmitter and receiver.

transmitter - a device that sends out radio or TV signals.

transparent - fine or sheer enough to see through.

treaty - a written contract between two or more political authorities.

typefounder - a person who designs and produces metal type for manual printing.

vellum - fine-grained animal skin used to write on.

video cassette recorder - a device that records video images on tapes called video cassettes.

visible - something you can see.

watermark - a mark on paper made by pressure of a design that is visible when held up to light.

word processor - a keyboard-operated terminal with a video monitor and magnetic storage used for producing typewritten documents.

zinc plate - a metal plate that has a protective coating of zinc, a metallic element.

INTERNET SITES

100 Years of Radio
http://www.alpcom.it/hamradio/
This Web site details the history of radio, from Guglielmo Marconi's work to modern broadcasting in the 1990s. It includes many links to radio Web sites around the world.

The Bell Institute
http://bell.uccb.ns.ca/
The Bell Institute of Sydney, Nova Scotia, is dedicated to the memory of Dr. Alexander Graham Bell, who lived, worked, and died in Canada. Their educational Web site has a kids page and is upgraded and sustained by the Electrical Engineering students of the University College of Cape Breton. Play games, conduct simple experiments designed by Bell, and view hundreds of images from the Image Gallery.

The Computer Museum History Center
http://www.computerhistory.org/index.page
Established in 1996, the Computer Museum History Center in Mountain View, California, is a nonprofit entity dedicated to the preservation and celebration of computing history. It is home to one of the largest collections of computing artifacts in the world.

The MZTV Museum
http://www.mztv.com/mztv.html
This site is devoted to the technological history of the TV receiver and its impact on the world. It has plenty of images illustrating the TV's evolution.

The Lascaux Grotto
http://www.culture.gouv.fr/culture/arcnat/lascaux/en/index4.html
This site offers a virtual tour of the famous Lascaux Grotto, home of the most beautiful Paleolithic-painted cave in the world. The Grotto contains more than 1,500 pictures of animals, all of which were painted between 15,000 and 13,000 B.C.

These sites are subject to change. Go to your favorite search engine and type in "communication" for more sites.

FOR FURTHER READING

Ganeri, Anita. *The Story of Writing and Printing.* New York: Evans Brothers Ltd., 1996.
———. *The Story of Communications.* New York: Oxford University Press, 1998.
Harness, Cheryl. *They're Off! The Story of the Pony Express.* New York: Simon & Schuster, 1996.
Jay, Michael. *The History of Communications.* New York: Thomson Learning, 1995.
Northrup, Mary. *American Computer Pioneers.* Springfield, N.J.: Enslow Publishers Inc., 1998.
Riehecky, Janet. *Television.* Tarrytown, N.Y.: Marshall Cavendish, Inc., 1996.

INDEX

C
camcorder 38, 39
cave paintings 4, 6
compact disc 38, 39, 41
  Russell, James T. 39
computer 5, 28-32, 34-40
  Apple
    Apple 1 37
    Jobs, Steve 37
    Macintosh 38
    Wayne, Ron 37
    Wozniak, Stephen 37
  ABC
    Atanasoff, John 29
    Berry, Clifford 29
  EDVAC 32
  ENIAC 31, 32
    Mauchly, John 31, 32
  floppy disk
    Shugart, Alan 37
  hand-held 40
  IBM
    laser printer 37
    Mark I 31
    PC 38
  laptop 38
  microchip 32
    Kilby, Jack St. Clair 32
  microprocessor 37
  Microsoft
    Allen, Paul 37
    Gates, Bill 37
    Windows 38
  minicomputer 35
  mouse 35, 38
    Engelbart, Douglas 35, 38
  operating system 35, 38
  personal computers 5, 37, 38
  Remington Rand
    UNIVAC 32
  supercomputer
    Cray-1 37

D
Digital Video Disc (DVD) 41

F
fax machine 35

H
hearing aid 14, 21
  audiophone
    Rhodes, R.G. 21
  ear trumpet 14, 21

I
Internet 5, 34, 35, 38-40
  email 5, 35, 40

L
language 4, 6
libraries 11
  Bibliothèque du Roi 11
  King Charles V 11

M
motion pictures 21-23, 26, 28, 32, 33
  3-D 33
  animation
    Disney, Walt 28
  Cinerama 33
  documentary
    Flaherty, Robert J. 26

motion pictures (continued)
  kinetoscope 21
    Dickson, William K.L. 21
    Edison, Thomas Alva 21
  newsreel
    Pathé, Charles 23
  nickelodeon
    Davis, Harry 23
    Harris, John P. 23
  talkies 26
  Technicolor 28

P
pager 5, 26, 32, 36
paper 4, 6, 7, 9, 10, 15, 18
  papyrus 7
  parchment 7
  rolled
    Robert, Nicholas-Louis 15
    Ts'ai Lun 7
  vellum 9
  watermark 10
phonograph 20, 23, 30, 39
  Berliner, Emile 23
  discs
    shellac 23
    vinyl 30, 39
  Edison, Thomas Alva 20
photocopying
  Carlson, Chester 29
  Kornei, Otto 29
  photocopier 28, 29, 32, 33
photography 17, 21, 23, 24, 28, 30, 31, 34, 40, 41
  camera 21, 23, 24, 30, 31, 34, 40, 41
  35mm
    Barnack, Oskar 24
  digital 40, 41
  Eastman, George 21, 23
    Brownie 23
    Kodak box 21
  Land, Edwin Herbert 31
    Polaroid 30, 31, 34
  daguerreotype
    Daguerre, Louis Jacques Mandé 17
  film 21
  flash
    electronic 28
    Edgerton, Harold 28
  Niepce, Joseph Nicéphore 17
postal system 4, 6, 7, 9, 10, 14, 15, 18, 24, 34, 35, 38
  airmail 24
    Pequet, Henri 24
  transcontinental service 24
  American 14, 15
    Franklin, Benjamin 15
  cursus publicus 7
  homing pigeons 4, 9
  messengers 4, 7, 10
    Pony Express 18
  post and relay system 7
  Taxis family 10
  ZIP codes 34, 35
  ZIP + 4 38
printing 4, 5, 8, 12, 13, 15, 16, 18, 21, 26
  color
    Fust, Johann 12
  ink, oil-based 12
  lithography
    Senefelder, Alois 15

printing (continued)
  magazines 4, 5, 26, 27
  newspapers 5, 14, 17, 26
    Associated Press 17
    Verhoeven, Abraham 14
  printing press
    Caxton, William 12
    cylinder
      Bauer, Andreas 16
      Koenig, Friedrich 16
    Gutenberg, Johannes 5, 12
      the Gutenberg Bible 12
    rotary
      Hoe, Richard M. 16, 18
    rotary web-fed
      Bullock, William 18
  typesetting
    Linotype machine
      Mergenthaler, Ottmar 21
  movable type
    clay 8
    metal 12
    Pi Sheng 8, 12
  typefounder 13

R
radio 22, 24-27, 32, 34
  AM 34
  car
    Galvin, Paul 27
  commercial broadcasting 25
  distress call
    CQD 22
    S.O.S. 22
  FM 34
  Hertz, Heinrich Rudolf 22
  Marconi, Guglielmo 22
  Radio Act of 1912 25
  shortwave 25
  transatlantic signal 22
  transistor 32
record keeping
  quipu 8

S
satellite 5, 32-34, 38, 39
  direct broadcast 5
  Intelsat 34, 39
  Telstar 34
sign language
  l'Epeé, Abbé Charles-Michel de 15
signals 4, 9, 13-16, 26, 27
  beacon 13
  Chappe, Claude 15
  drum 4
  smoke 4, 9
  telescope 14, 15
    Galilei, Galileo 14
    Lippershey, Hans 14
  traffic 26, 27
    Morgan, Garrett Augustus 27

T
tape recorder
  Poulsen, Valdimar 28
telegraph 15, 17-19, 26
  Cook, Sir William F. 17
  Morse, Samuel 17

telegraph (continued)
  Morse Code 17
  photograph transmission 26
  stock ticker
    Calahan, E.A. 19
  teletype machine 26
  transatlantic cable 19
  transcontinental 18
  Wheatstone, Sir Charles 17
telephone 5, 20, 24, 25, 32, 34-36, 38
  Bell, Alexander Graham 20, 25
  cellular 5, 38
  fiber optics 36, 38
  rotary dial 35
  speakerphone 32
  touch tone 35
  transaction 36
  transmission
    transatlantic 25
    transcontinental 24, 25
  Watson, Thomas 20, 25
television 27-30, 40, 41
  commercial 30
  Farnsworth, Philo 27, 29
  HDTV 41
transistor 22, 30, 32
  Bardeen, John 30
  Brattain, Walter Houser 30
  Shockley, William Bradford 30
typewriter 19, 23, 34-36
  electric 23
    Edison, Thomas Alva 23
  Glidden, Carlos 19
  QWERTY 19
  shift key 19
  Sholes, Christopher 19
  Soulé, Samuel 19

V
vacuum tube 22, 31
  De Forest, Lee 22
videotape recorder 33, 36
  Betamax 36
  VHS 36

W
word processor 36
World War I 24, 25
World War II 29, 30
writing 4, 6, 8, 10, 11, 16
  book copiers 11
  braille 16
    Braille, Louis 16
  cuneiform 4, 6
  hieroglyphics
    Egyptian 6
    Mayan 8
  letters 10
  Rosetta Stone 6
    Champollion, Jean-François 6
  stationers 11
writing instruments 4, 21, 28, 29
  ball-point pen 28, 29
    Biro, Georg 29
    Biro, Ladislao 29
  fountain pen 21
    Waterman, L.E. 21